HOWARD G. HENDRICKS
WILLIAM D. HENDRICKS

LIVING
BY THE
BOOK
┤ VIDEO SERIES ├
┤ WORKBOOK ├

7-PART CONDENSED SERIES AND LEADER'S GUIDE

THE ART AND SCIENCE OF READING THE BIBLE

Published by Living By The Book, c/o The Giftedness Center, 3333 Lee Parkway, Suite 600, Dallas, Texas, 75219

www.livingbythebook.net

© Copyright 2010 by Howard G. Hendricks & William D. Hendricks.

Note: Throughout this workbook, wherever the masculine or feminine pronouns are used, they should be understood as indicating both genders, unless the context implies otherwise.

A WORD BEFORE YOU START...

You are about to embark on an adventure that will take you into territory uncharted for most Christians—the serious study of God's Word. Our journey begins with the first and most important skill of Bible study—Observation. Then we'll travel past the perils of Interpretation. Our ultimate goal—which should be the goal of every Christian—is Application, in which we practice biblical truth in order to become people who are *living* by The Book.

Your guide for this trip is Dr. Howard G. Hendricks, Distinguished Professor at Dallas Theological Seminary, and chairman of the seminary's Center for Christian Leadership. Dr. Hendricks is the author or coauthor of numerous books, including the best-selling Moody Press title that parallels this video series, *Living By the Book*.

Both the book and the video series are the fruit of more than fifty years of Dr. Hendricks teaching Bible study methods to thousands of seminary students and to tens of thousands of laypeople around the world.

Dr. Charles Swindoll, Chancellor of Dallas Theological Seminary and a man known internationally through his popular radio ministry, "Insight For Living," says of Dr. Hendricks, his friend and mentor, "The teaching of Howie Hendricks on how to study the Bible is beyond great. It is life-changing! How do I know? During my days in seminary, I drank in each word as I absorbed every session he taught. It changed my life. Not a week passes without my using some technique or principle that I learned from this gifted man."

Countless others have hailed Dr. Hendricks' Bible study methods with similar praise. Now this practical and life-changing approach has been video-recorded in order to help you get into God's Word for yourself.

The seven video sessions in "Living By The Book" show Dr. Hendricks leading a small group of people in a seminar format. This format allows for more interaction between student and teacher—and will also encourage your participation as a viewer. We've created this workbook to help you follow along in the video presentations, to give you helpful, hands-on exercises for practicing the principles presented, and to set before you a challenge—to become a person who *lives* by The Book.

Have a great journey!

CONTENTS

INTRODUCTION

HOW TO USE THIS WORKBOOK

This workbook has been designed and written expressly for use with the seven-part video series, "Living By The Book," featuring Dr. Howard Hendricks. The aim of the series—as well as this workbook—is not just to make you more aware of your need for personal Bible study, but to actively move you into actual Bible study.

For some, this workbook may seem mildly task-oriented or "academic." If so, that is somewhat by intention. It's not that we want to discourage anyone from studying the Bible. Just the opposite: we want to encourage everyone to acquire the skills and tools needed to dig deeply into God's Word, in order to find the many treasures waiting to be discovered. But it's a fact that the rewards of studying the Bible come in direct proportion to the time and effort invested in the task, as well as from the use of a proven method for understanding and applying Scripture.

Each session in this workbook contains three sections of material—one for preparation, one for following along with Dr. Hendricks, and one for putting into practice the principles he covers. Here's an overview:

PREPARING FOR THE BOOK

STEP ONE: Open Mind
This is a challenge to prepare yourself mentally, by considering a few choice quotes and Bible verses that highlight the theme of each session.

STEP TWO: Open Heart
This is a challenge to prepare yourself spiritually, to open your heart and life to the scrutiny of God's Word. As you'll quickly discover, the Bible cannot be our textbook without

becoming our life-book.

STEP THREE: Open Book

This is a challenge to prepare logistically to study God's Word. Throughout the Bible, we are given glimpses of people who knew the Scriptures as a result of careful, disciplined, and persistent study. They reaped valuable rewards as a result of that study. With that in mind, this section offers helpful hints and how-to's for the person who wants a similar quality in their own study of Scripture.

LOOKING TO THE BOOK

[THE RECORDED SESSION WILL BE STARTED HERE]

In this section, Dr. Hendricks' videotaped presentation will be outlined, with blanks left for you to fill in as you follow along. There's also plenty of room in the margins for you to write down notes, thoughts, and other material as you watch and listen. Having the flow of each message will give you a valuable tool for future reference.

[THE RECORDED SESSION WILL END HERE]

WORKING IN THE BOOK

Now we come to the section where the benefits of "Living By The Book" stand or fall! Unless you faithfully work through each "Working in the Book" section, this video series may become just another memory.

On the other hand, if you are diligent to complete each exercise and assignment as best you can, based on Dr. Hendricks' material, you will find—as countless others have—that the pages of Scripture will open up to you, and the Bible will have its intended, life-changing effect on your life.

One final note: we've provided three levels of exercises, as follows:

LEVEL ONE: Let's Get Started

Level One is designed for people who are just beginning the process of personal Bible study. It asks them to interact with the material in much the same way as the participants in the recorded session interacted with Dr. Hendricks. There will also be questions dealing with biblical content, study methods, and other discovery skills.

LEVEL TWO: For Those Who Want More

Level Two is designed for those who are already familiar with some of the methods discussed and want more "in-depth" challenges. In addition to revisiting some aspects of the lesson content, these exercises will encourage participants to make their own discoveries in Scripture in order to build their confidence and provide them with an opportunity for personal interaction with the Word.

LEVEL THREE: Building Beyond the Foundation

Level Three is designed for those who simply cannot stop once they have experienced the joy of effective, first-hand study of the Word. These exercises provide even more opportunities by taking participants to more challenging passages of Scripture. They also highlight the application of Bible study skills for those who are ready to strike out on their own.

CONCLUSION

If you find yourself or your group going through the "Living By The Book" series more than once, try taking on a higher level of exercises the second or third time around.

Also, if you think of ways that this workbook could be made more effective and helpful to others, feel free to write us at Living By The Book, c/o The Giftedness Center, 3333 Lee Parkway, Suite 600, Dallas, Texas, 75219.

May God bless you in your diligent study of His Word!

OBSERVATION
What Do I See?

NOTES

SESSION ONE
AN OVERVIEW OF THE PROCESS

PREPARING FOR THE BOOK

STEP ONE: Open Mind

- Did you know that the Bible is not simply one book? It is 66 books in one, composed and compiled by more than 40 human authors over a period of more than 1,600 years. Its human writers included kings, fishermen, diplomats, prophets, shepherds, lawyers, doctors, soldiers, historians, and many others.

  Furthermore, the Bible addresses hundreds of subjects, including life, death, God, marriage, the family, worship, truth, and eternity. Yet despite its many authors and countless topics, the Bible is in perfect harmony from cover to cover, is entirely consistent within itself, and proves its supernatural origins through its supernatural unity.

- In spite of being the most persecuted book in history, the Bible is also the most widely published and the best-selling volume of all time.

- "The family Bible is more often used to adorn coffee tables or press flowers than it is to feed souls and discipline lives." — *Charles Colson*

STEP TWO: Open Heart

- "How can a young man keep his way pure? By living according to your word. . . . I have hidden your word in my heart that I might not sin against you." —*Psalm 119:9, 11*

- In John 17:17, Jesus prayed to the Father concerning all His disciples: "Sanctify them by the truth; your word is truth."

- "Men do not reject the Bible because it contradicts itself, but because it contradicts them." —*E. Paul Hovey*

- "For the word of God is living and active, sharper than any double-edged sword, it penetrates even to dividing soul and spirit, joints and marrow; it judges the thoughts and attitudes of the heart." — *Hebrews 4:12*

- History tells us that when Crowfoot, the chief of the Blackfoot nation in southern Alberta, gave the Canadian Pacific Railway permission to lay track from Medicine Hat to Calgary, he was given in exchange a lifetime railroad pass. Reportedly, Crowfoot put the pass in a leather pouch and wore it around his neck for the rest of his life—but he never once availed himself of the rights and privileges it spelled out.

  What a tragedy it is when Christians do the same thing with the Word of God, using it as a decorative badge of Christianity, but never availing themselves of the wealth of access to God's thoughts that it affords.

- While it is true that we must approach the Word of God with an open mind, we also must recognize that God's truth provides absolute boundaries for that openness. As G.K. Chesterton has said, "Merely having an open mind is nothing. The object of opening the mind, as of opening the mouth, is to shut it again on something solid."

- Before you begin this life-changing study, ask God to open your understanding, to give you insight into His eternal Word, and to create in your heart not only a genuine hunger for Scripture, but a relentless diligence to study it carefully and accurately in order to obey Him.

STEP THREE: Open Book

If you are beginning this study as part of a group or class, you may not have to worry about an appropriate place to study God's Word; the group setting may provide that for you.

However, if you are setting out to study the Bible on your own—as a way of life—be sure to set aside not only the time for Bible study, but also a suitable place.

Many find that a regular time each morning is ideal for a "quiet time" with God. If mornings are not good for you, consider reserving a portion of time during the day, such as your lunch hour, or 30 minutes in the evening after everything at home has quieted down.

Regardless of when you meet with God, be faithful to the time and come expecting to learn from Him. Try to avoid interruptions and distractions, and keep in mind the suggestions we'll be offering in the lessons ahead.

If you want your time of Bible study to be effective, come with:

- **A pencil or pen.** Be prepared to make notes and write down what you learn.

- **Paper.** Write down your thoughts and findings in a format that provides easy access, such as a journal, file folder, or notebook. Don't be afraid to write in the margins of your Bible.

- **Purpose.** Always come to God's Word expecting Him to teach you and to change your life.

- **Prayer.** Never begin your study without first talking to the Author, asking Him to open your heart and mind, and submitting yourself to Him as the great Teacher.

LOOKING TO THE BOOK

[BEGIN SESSION ONE]

Introduction

- "The Bible will keep you from _____ *Sin* _____

  or _____ *Sin* _____ will keep you from

the ___*book*___ ."

- It is a tragedy that many Christians today are ___*Many christen are under*___ the Word of God, but they are not ___*in it*___ for themselves.

- Being under the Word of God should be a ___*stimulus*___ _____, not a ___*substitute*___, for getting into it for ourselves.

I. Two Basic Questions to Answer

A. Question One:

"Why is it that people do not study the Bible?"

1. They do not put it on their ___*priority list*___.

2. They believe it is not ___*not relevant*___ for today.

3. They do not know how to ___*begin to get into*___ *it fulfill* ~~to study it~~.

4. They do not think they can *study or* ___*understand*___ it on their own.

B. Question Two:

"Why must we study the Bible?"

Let's consider three passages:

1. 1 Peter 2:2

Heb 5 11–15

- The first reason we discover in the Bible for studying the Scriptures is that ___*Only mean of spiritual growth*___ There is no ___*growth*___, spiritually, apart from ___*Word of God*___.

- We should grab for the Word just like a baby grabs for a bottle.

- We need to acquire a taste for God's Word. We do that by spending time in it.

- The goal of Bible study is that we might grow — not know. We can't grow without knowing, but we can know without growing.

> *"The Bible was not written to satisfy your curiosity, but to make you conform to Christ's image. Not to make you a smarter sinner, but to make you like the Savior. Not to fill your head with a collection of biblical facts, but to transform your life."*

2. Hebrews 5:11-14

- The second reason we discover why we must study the Bible is that it is the divine means of developing *spiritual maturity*

- Who are the "mature"? The mature are those who by constant use have trained themselves by taking the Word of God and using it in their lives to distinguish good from evil.

- The highest mark of spiritual maturity is not how much you understand, it is how much you use.

- The opposite of ignorance in the spiritual realm is not knowledge, it is obedience.

3. 2 Timothy 3:16-17

This passage tells us that Scripture is profitable for four things:

- **doctrine, or teaching.** It will structure your thinking.

- **rebuke.** It will tell you when you are out of bounds.

- **correction.** It will not only reveal your sin, it also provides the dynamic whereby you can conform to God's will.

- **training in righteous living.** It is God's means of showing you how to live.

> *"I said to a group of businessmen some time ago, 'If you didn't know any more about your business or profession than you know about Christianity after the same number of years of exposure, what would happen?' One guy said, 'They'd ship me!' I said, 'Thank, you, sir, for the honesty.'"*

- Why do we need to study God's Word? We have seen three basic reasons:

    1. It is essential to __Grow__ .

    2. It is essential to __maturity__ .

    3. It is essential for __equipping you & training you__

II. What Bible Study Involves

> *"A problem well defined is a problem half-solved."*
> *— Charles Kettering*

Methodical

We are going to define Bible study with three progressive statements:

A. Bible study is __Methodicalness__ .

- It involves taking certain __steps__ in a certain __order__ to guarantee a certain __result__ .

- It involves both a __product__ and a __process__ .

1. The product is. . .
    a. __personal study__ of the Scriptures.
    b. Study that produces __life change__ .

2. The process involves a _____*three*_____ -step approach.

   a. The first step is _____*Observation*_____ .
   This is where you ask and answer the question,
   "What do I _____*see (looking for details)*_____ ?"

   b. The second step is _____*interpretation*_____ .
   This is where you ask and answer the question,
   "What does it _____*central quest info for meaning*_____ ?"

   c. The third step is _____*application*_____ .
   This is where you ask and answer the question,
   "How does it _____*work*_____ ?"

B. Bible study is *methodicalness* with a view to becoming
_____*receptive*_____ and _____*reproductive*_____ .

> "The Bible is relevant because it is revealed.
> It is always a return to reality."

- Before we can ever make an impact on our generation,
  the Scripture has to make an impact upon
  _____*our life*_____ .

- There are two aspects to effective living:
  1. _____*Involved*_____ in the world.
  2. _____*Isolated*_____ from the world.

C. Bible study is *methodicalness* with a view to becoming
receptive and reproductive by means of _____*1st hand*_____
_____*knowledge / acquaintance*_____ .

III. An Overview of the Process

Term - track

A. Step One: Observation: "What do I see?"

There are basically four things to look for:

1. _Terms_

   Not words. _terms_ have specific meaning based on their context.

2. _Structure (gramatical)_ _subject_ _object_ _main Verb_

   There are two basic kinds:

   a. _gramatical_ lets us know important information like subject, object, and main verbs.

   b. _literary_ _structure_ reveals clues through recognition of things like questions and answers, cause-and-effect, and so on.

3. _literary form_

   This tells us whether we are looking at poetry, narrative, history, or prophecy.

4. _Atmosphere_

   This reveals feeling, mood, tone, and environment. What was it like to be in the author's shoes?

B. Step Two: Interpretation: "What does it mean?"

Three things will help us discover the meaning of a passage:

1. Bombard the text with _Questions_. The Bible is never embarrassed to be asked _questn_.

2. Look for the _answers_. These most often will come out of your observational process.

3. Seek to _Integrate_ the parts and _Put them together_. Put all the details together into a meaningful whole.

> *"The more time you spend in observation, the less time you will spend in interpretation, and the more accurate will be your results. The less time you spend in observation, the more time you will spend in interpretation, and the less accurate will be your results."*

C. Step Three: Application: "How does it work?"

There are two things to look for in this process:

1. How does it work for ___*for me*___ ?

2. How does it work for ___*for others*___ ?

How would this transform lives?

This is the overview of where we are going. Don't miss the exciting journey!

[END OF SESSION ONE]

WORKING IN THE BOOK

LEVEL ONE: Let's Get Started

1a. Which of the reasons for not studying God's Word most closely fits your experience? *Busyness*

1b. Which of the reasons for studying the Bible best answers this?

2. Read 1 Peter 2:2. How would you characterize your desire for the "pure milk" of God's Word?

3. Based on Hebrews 5:11-14, how would you evaluate your spiritual maturity?

4. Read 2 Timothy 3:16-17. Can you give a concrete example of where you need to experience these traits of God's Word in your life? What does that reveal about the value of Scripture for you?

5. What are the three steps in the process of Bible study and the questions each is designed to answer? *open mind – Spiritual growth, open heart – open to receive guidance & be a true follower of God and sharing the word, open Book – be in the word training with others particularly the last.*

6. Why is it necessary to take the three steps of Bible study method in order? *If our mind is not open to learning, hearts open, etc then we are not going to grow, growing in love of god be able to spread the word to those who are lost.*

7. What do you most look forward to as you get started in the process of personal Bible study? *growth in all areas*

LEVEL TWO: For Those Who Want More

1. What do we learn about the Word of God from each of the following passages?

   - Psalm 119:105 *the word gives us vision to see the way God is guiding us.*
   - Romans 12:1-2 *Give our all to God be willing to listen to God carry out his leadership in my/our lives*
   - Jeremiah 15:16 *We are to joyfully study the word as his children. The word is food for our soul*
   - 2 Timothy 2:15 *We are to conduct our lives in a manner that is evident to all that we are a follower of Christ.*

2. Following the statement of Hebrews 5:11-14, what is the call of Hebrews 6:1a? How would you phrase this in your own words? How would you accomplish it? *Prioritize my time and efforts to spend more time in the Word to mature in my faith to a greater extent*

3. The phrase "inspired by God" (2 Timothy 3:16) literally means God-breathed. What does this reveal about the Word of God? *It is "the" guidance direct from God that we are to use in living out lives and carrying out his will for us*

4. What does Acts 17:11 reveal about the "methodicalness" with which the Berean believers studied Scripture? *greatly eager to study Gods word to see if what they were told was true.*

5. What do the following passages indicate that the outcome of Bible study will be?

   - 1 John 5:3-4 *Knowing the guidance God gives to be able to overcome the temptation that their lives gives that could pull us away from following Gods direction*
   - Romans 12:2 *Be able to overcome the worlds evil pattern, able to recognize God's voice in giving us direction.*
   - Colossians 3:16-17 *Whatever we do accomplish in the name of the lord, give him thanks*

6. What do you learn about the importance of individual terms in Scripture from Matthew 5:18 and Matthew 24:35? *Gods Word is set firm til Christ return. Our New Covenant*

New Covenant Love God Love others as yourself

7. In regard to the step of Application, what do you learn from Jeremiah 15:16?

LEVEL THREE: Building Beyond the Foundation

1. What "cycle" or ongoing progression can you find in Paul's prayer in Colossians 1:9-10? Diagram it if possible.

   my Pray ⊘ ☺ ☺ ☺ — grow in Knowledge of God

2. Besides "Thy word," find at least seven other names that the psalmist uses to describe the Word of God in Psalm 119. What differences do you think these names imply? What makes them similar? *Law, statutes, precepts, decrees, commands, Word, way of truth, promises they are gods directions to us but they are also gods "words" to us*

3. Write your own definition for each of the three steps of Bible study.

4. What do you think would be the dangers of...

   • Interpretation without observation?

   • Application without interpretation?

5. Read 1 Corinthians 2:14–3:3. What three types of people are described, and what will be the relationship of each to the Word of God? What does this reveal about personal prerequisites for understanding the Bible? *unsaved, Spiritual man, Worldly ↓ ↓ ↓ No relationsip Need growth not fully devoted*

6. What literary form (narrative, poetry, history, wisdom, prophecy) would you generally expect to find in:

   • The Psalms – *poetry*

   • Luke – *narrative*

   • Joshua – *history*

   • Proverbs – *wisdom*

• Acts — history

• Revelation — prophecy

7. How would you answer someone who says that 2 Peter 1:20-21 teaches that we cannot understand or interpret the Bible for ourselves? If possible, support your answer with Scripture.

SESSION TWO
LEARNING TO LOOK, LEARNING TO READ

PREPARING FOR THE BOOK

STEP ONE: Open Mind

- Billy Graham was once asked, "If you had to live your life over again, what would you do differently?" Graham replied, "One of my great regrets is that I have not studied enough. I wish I had studied more and preached less. People have pressured me into speaking to groups, when I should have been studying and preparing."

- "By wisdom a house is built, and through understanding it is established." —*Proverbs 24:3*

- It has been said that the Bible is so deep that theologians cannot touch the bottom, yet so shallow that babes cannot drown.

STEP TWO: Open Heart

- "Jesus answered, 'It is written: "Man does not live on bread alone, but on every word that comes from the mouth of God."'" —*Matthew 4:4 (see also Deuteronomy 8:3)*

- "Then Job replied to the Lord: 'I know that you can do all things; no plan of yours can be thwarted. You asked, "Who is this that obscures my counsel without knowledge?" Surely I spoke of things I did not understand, things too wonderful for me to know.'" —*Job 42:1-3*

- It has been said that God has given each of us six openings for taking in information, and only one for giving it out. That alone should tell us something!

- "Be still and know that I am God." —*Psalm 46:10*

- Before we begin this lesson, let's recognize our need to be quiet, to calm down, to listen to what God has to say, rather than being quick to speak our minds. Let's ask God to give us a pliable will and an attentive ear as we go to His Word in study.

STEP THREE: Open Book

TOOLS OF THE TRADE

A common question asked by people who are just beginning to study the Bible on their own is, "What books can I buy that will help me in my study?" Too often, the first ones they buy are *commentaries*, in which others publish the results of their study. But it would be better to buy tools that first help us dig deep on our own.

Throughout this workbook, suggestions will be made under the heading, "Tools of the Trade." For now, here are three suggestions:

- **A common, everyday dictionary.** It is amazing how much more we can learn when we understand what words mean!

- **A good Bible handbook,** such as *Eerdman's Bible Handbook.* A Bible handbook presents basic information about each book, usually in the same order as the biblical books. It also provides useful facts about the history, culture, and customs pertaining to the biblical text.

- **An exhaustive concordance,** such as *Strong's* or *Young's*, or the one published for the translation of study Bible you are using.

  Don't let the size of a concordance scare you. A concordance is just a list of all the words used in the Bible. Once you learn to use a concordance, it can help you not only find passages that are "on the tip of your tongue," but to trace particular words, people, and places throughout the biblical text.

LOOKING TO THE BOOK

[BEGIN SESSION TWO]

Introduction

- The first step in the process of Bible study methods is
  Observation _Learn how to read better &_
  faster.

- The only difference between any two people is how much
  they ___see___ in the same cubic foot of space.
  The ability to ___observe___ is a developed process.

- There are two basic reasons why we don't get more from
  our study of Scripture:
  1. We don't know how to ___read___.
  2. We don't know what to ___look for___.

In this lesson we are going to examine three basic rules for
reading the Bible.

I. **Rule #1: Learn to read** ___better and faster___.

- There is a direct correlation between your ___efficient___
  in reading and your_____ in Bible study.

TOOLS OF THE TRADE

How to Read a Book, by Mortimer J. Adler

II. **Rule #2: Learn to read** ___as if for the first time___.

A good suggestion for reading the Word of God freshly is
to read it in several different ___Versions___.

III. **Rule #3: Learn to read it as a** ___love letter___
_____.

- We need to come to the Word of God in love with the
  Person who wrote it.

[END OF SESSION TWO]

Handwritten notes (right margin):

Mortimer J. Adly
How to read a book NOTES
Pocket Knife
slide rule
Pencil
Crescent Wrench
Spool of thread
fisherman paperweight

11 times Jesus said Do
you not know how to read

Read as like the first time

WORKING IN THE BOOK

LEVEL ONE: Let's Get Started

1. What was the psalmist's request in Psalm 119:18? What was he fundamentally asking for?

   Guidance for a blessed and fulfilling life

2. By what means can the wisdom and knowledge of Proverbs be obtained, according to Proverbs 22:17-21 (note v. 20)?

   by paying attention, listening and applying to our hearts.

3. What do you think Jesus meant when He talked about those with "ears to hear" (see Matthew 11:15; 13:9, 43; Luke 14:35)? How does this relate to our need to "learn how to read" the Bible?

   Those who have "heard the Word are to be disciples to share the word with others" whether believer or unbeliever.

4. What was the main action that brought about great consequences in 2 Chronicles 34:14-15, 18-21?

   Returning the "Law" to the people of Israel

5. In what way was Joshua supposed to read the Word of God, according to Joshua 1:8? What was to be the result?

   Meditate on it day and night, + do not stray from it. Result, prosper + be successful

LEVEL TWO: For Those Who Want More

1. Set aside a time to read all of the Gospel of Mark in one sitting, without interruption. After you have finished, answer the following questions:

   • What obstacles did you have to overcome in order to read Mark straight through?

   • What new insights into this gospel did you gain from reading it all at once?

- In what ways do you think this reading would help you study Mark in detail?

2. Read the following verses in at least three different versions (or translations). Does anything about each verse strike you differently as a result of seeing it in a new light?

- Hebrews 4:12-13

- Ephesians 5:15-19

- Matthew 6:19-24

3. List at least five similarities between the way a person tends to read a love letter and the way we should approach God's Word.

4. Based on John 1:1-18, why does a parallel exist between our love for Jesus Christ and our love for the Word of God? How should this affect our desire to read His Word carefully?

LEVEL THREE: Building Beyond the Foundation

1. Read Matthew 12:1-8. What was the answer to Jesus' question, "Have you not read. . . ?" What would say was the religious leaders' problem? Be specific.

2. In Psalm 119, find no fewer than ten verses that reflect the psalmist's attitude in approaching, before applying, God's Word. What effect do you think his approach had on his application?

3. Using an English dictionary, provide a brief definition for some of the words that are used in the Bible to describe the way the psalmist approached God's Word:

   • Meditate

   • Observe

   • Cleave to

   • Seek

   • Long for

   • Delight in

   • Regard

   • Consider

   • Esteem

   • Keep

   • Love

4. Re-phrase Psalm 119:18 into your own personal prayer concerning the way you approach God's Word.

SESSION THREE

LEARNING WHAT TO LOOK FOR

PREPARING FOR THE BOOK

STEP ONE: Open Mind

- Most of us are familiar with the Pony Express and its oft-romanticized contribution to the history of the Old West. But for all its glamour, the Pony Express was a business enterprise—and was run like one.

  To ferry mail across the open expanse of the western territories, the express route ran 1,900 miles from St. Joseph, Missouri to Sacramento, California. The trip was made in about 10 days, using 40 men who each raced about 50 miles, riding a total of 500 fine horses in the process.

  To conserve weight, riders wore light clothing, rode on extremely small saddles, and carried no weapons. Their mail pouches were also compact and lightweight. Letters cost $5 per ounce for postage.

  Yet for all these efficiencies in terms of weight, one thing was not sacrificed: every rider carried a full-size Bible, presented to him when he joined the Pony Express.

  By contrast, how often are we found without the Word of God at our side, in our day of comfort and convenience?

- "This is how we know that we love the children of God: by loving God and carrying out his commands."—*1 John 5:2*

- During the period of intellectual history called the Enlightenment, a philosophy known as *deism* was sweeping Europe. In the midst of this development, the famous skeptic, Voltaire, proclaimed that within 25 years, the Bible would be forgotten and Christianity would be a thing of the past.

However, 40 years after Voltaire's death in 1778, the Bible and other Christian literature were being printed in what had once been Voltaire's own house!

- "The grass withers and the flowers fall, because the breath of the LORD blows on them."—*Isaiah 40:7*

- Martin Luther is reported to have said concerning his own study of the Scriptures: "I study my Bible as I gather apples. First, I shake the whole tree that the ripest might fall. Then I shake each limb, and when I have shaken each limb, I shake each branch and every twig. Then I look under every leaf. I shake the Bible as a whole, like shaking the whole tree. Then I shake every limb—study book after book. Then I shake every branch, giving attention to the chapters when they do not break the sense. Then I shake every twig, or a careful study of the paragraphs and sentences and words and their meanings."

- "Anyone who listens to the word but does not do what it says is like a man who looks at his face in a mirror and, after looking at himself, goes away and immediately forgets what he looks like. But the man who looks intently into the perfect law that gives freedom, and continues to do this, not forgetting what he has heard, but doing it—he will be blessed in what he does." —*James 1:23-25*

- **Fast Fact:** Out of approximately 667 recorded prayers in the Bible, there are about 454 recorded answers.

- As you open God's Word to study how to study it, spend a minute or two examining your life in the perfect light of that Word. If God reveals sin in your life, deal with it now on the basis of 1 John 1:9—that your study of Him and His truth might not be hindered.

STEP THREE: Open Book

> **TOOLS OF THE TRADE**
>
> *A Dictionary of Synonyms and Antonyms,* by Joseph Devlin.
>   Why is this little book so helpful? Because we Christians often fall into a pattern of using Christian terminology and jargon that keeps us from making the crucial connection between what we observe in God's Word and where we live in this world. A tool that offers a variety of parallel or contrasting words can effectively snap us out of that mode and open up our perspective.

LOOKING TO THE BOOK

[BEGIN SESSION THREE]

Introduction

- By way of review, we have already seen that there are two essential components to quality observation:

  1. We must learn how to _Open minded / better of faster_

  2. We must learn how to _open heart / as for the first term_

- In this lesson we will deal with the second of these two components.

- Like a doctor who knows what to look for in a patient, we need to know what to look for when coming to God's Word. Let's consider six things to look for:

I. Look for things that are _____.

The Spirit of God uses a number of ways to do this, including:

A. The amount of _____

B. The stated _____.

C. The _____ of the material.

D. Movement from the _____
to the _____.

II. Look for things that are _____.

- These may be terms, phrases, or clauses.

    Examples:

- Psalm 136

- Hebrews 11

- Others:

III. Look for things that are _____.

The biblical authors may show in a number of ways:

A. Movement from the _____
to the _____.

    Example:

B. _____.

    Example:

C. _____.

    Example:

IV. Look for things that are _____.

• Expressions to look for: _____

_____.

Example:

V. Look for things that are _____.

• Key word: " _____ "

Example:

VI. Look for things that are _____.

Examples:

• Abraham

• Moses

• David

• Peter

• John Mark

> *"People have not changed.*
> *Believers in the Bible are just like us!"*

[END OF SESSION THREE]

NOTES

WORKING IN THE BOOK

LEVEL ONE: Let's Get Started

1. In what way does God emphasize the importance of people, and specifically the descendants of Abraham, in the Book of Genesis?

2. What key concept is communicated through repetition in...

   • Hebrews 11 *faith in God in all things*

   • Psalm 150 *praise God for his greatness*

   • 1 Corinthians 13 *Love (a gift of the holy Spirit)*

3. What development of relationship do you find in Ephesians 5:10-11, 13-18? *seek the lords will and make use of every opportunity to bring light to Gods message*

4. What does James use to get his point across in James 2:14-17; 3:13; 4:1-4? *Our faith will be shown in how we joyfully serve/help others.*

5. What similar circumstances are unbelievers among believers compared to in Jude 4-8, 11?

6. What contrast is emphasized in 2 Corinthians 6:14-18? How is this contrast established? *a person saying they are believers but do not act accordingly. there is not middle ground ... you must be all in*

LEVEL TWO: For Those Who Want More

1. Read each of the following passages, then briefly explain what is being emphasized and how that emphasis is established:

   • John 17 *Christ prays for believers he is leaving behind as he ascends into heaven.*

   • Proverbs 3 *Keep gods commandments for a long life. Honor god in every area of our lives and he will provide for us*

   • Ephesians 1 *there is a time Unknown to man when we ca now longer recieve the Gift of Salvation offered to man.*

2. In Psalm 119, we find emphasis by the amount of space devoted to this psalm (it is the longest of all the psalms) and also through repetition. Briefly summarize what is being emphasized and what you think that indicates.
   Study the word, meditate on it apply it to our every action

3. Summarize the comparisons found in each of the following passages:

   • Psalm 127:3-5 *Children are a blessing from God.*

   • Genesis 15:5 *Abraham was to father many children despite his age & a barren wife... father of Many Nations*

   • Ephesians 5:22-23 *husband are to be the head of the family giving guidance in mutual respect between husband & wife*

   • Psalm 61:3 *God is our "Go to person"*

4. Trace the contrast established and explained in Galatians 5:19-23. Can you simplify this contrast into a chart?

5. What do you find particularly "true to life" in the following passages?

   • Matthew 1:18-25

   • Nehemiah 5:1-13 *the have & have nots. Sometime the wealthy seek gain in all areas at the expense of those who are struggling to survive*

   • 2 Samuel 11:1-5 *we have consequences for not honoring the commandments"*

   • Mark 14:66-72 *We don't always acknowledge what is true.*

LEVEL THREE: Building Beyond the Foundation

Without using any of the passages listed in Session Three or in the questions above, find at least three examples in Scripture (and provide a brief explanation) of each of the following:

1. Emphasis through the amount of space devoted to the topic.

2. Emphasis through movement from the lesser to the greater.

3. Repetition of terms, phrases, or clauses.

4. Ideas or concepts related through movement from the general to the specific, question-and-answer, or cause-and-effect.

5. Ideas or concepts that are presented as alike or as opposites.

6. Episodes that are true to life and reveal the unchangeableness of truth or human nature.

NOTES

INTERPRETATION
What Does It Mean?

SESSION FOUR
CONTENT & CONTEXT

PREPARING FOR THE BOOK

STEP ONE: Open Mind

- "Do your best to present yourself to God as one approved, a workman who does not need to be ashamed and who correctly handles the word of truth." —*2 Timothy 2:15*

- "One of the reasons mature people stop learning is that they become less and less willing to risk failure." —*John W. Gardner*

- "The Word of God is not a rubber nose that you can twist to suit your face." —*Earl Radmacher*

- "Above all, you must understand that no prophecy of Scripture came about by the prophet's own interpretation. For prophecy never had its origin in the will of man, but men spoke from God as they were carried along by the Holy Spirit." —*2 Peter 1:20-21*

STEP TWO: Open Heart

- "Let the word of Christ dwell in you richly." —*Colossians 3:16a*

- "Our great problem is the problem of trafficking in un-lived truth. We try to communicate what we've never experienced in our own lives." —*D.L. Moody*

- "My rule for Christian living is this: anything that dims my vision of Christ, or takes away my taste for Bible study, or cramps my prayer life, or makes Christian work difficult is wrong for me, and I must, as a Christian, turn away from it." —*Dr. Wilbur Chapman*

• "In the sight of God, who gives life to everything, and of Christ Jesus, who while testifying before Pontius Pilate made the good confession, I charge you to keep this command without spot or blame until the appearing of our Lord Jesus Christ." —*1 Timothy 6:13-14*

STEP THREE: Open Book

We are now ready to move on to the second step of Bible study, Interpretation. As we will see, interpreting Scripture can be hard, serious work—but well worth the effort.

Before we launch into this step, it's important to recognize that it *is* possible to interpret the Bible confidently and accurately. In our "everything is relative" society, some Christians have given up the fight for biblical truth, assuming that "people can interpret the Bible any way they want." In other words, there really are no right or wrong answers in terms of what the Bible means.

But the Bible itself tells us something entirely different. In fact, read 2 Peter 1:20-21. You'll discover that it says we cannot interpret the Bible any way we want. Rather, our interpretation must square with the rest of Scripture, since the same Holy Spirit of God "moved" (or inspired) the authors during the process of writing God's Word.

Peter's statement is not a warning against interpreting Scripture, but an encouragement to always interpret Scripture by using Scripture, first and foremost. Our most valuable tool for interpreting and understanding any portion of the biblical text is the rest of the biblical text, taken in its historical and grammatical context, and using sound-minded, level-headed principles of interpretation—plus a healthy dose of common sense.

Dr. Hendricks will cover this principle in more detail as he continues in our video study of Bible study methods.

LOOKING TO THE BOOK

[BEGIN SESSION FOUR]

Introduction

- Some people, knowing nothing about Christianity, think that Christian faith is a matter of _taking a deep breath_ what we know is not true.

- When you become a Christian, you do not shift your mind into _interpretation_ .

- In this session, we begin to turn our attention to the second major step in Bible study methods, the step of _observation_ .

Note the connection between the two:

- In Observation we asked, "What do I _see_ ?"

- In Interpretation we ask, "What does it _mean_ ?"

- In Observation we _excavate_ .

- In Interpretation we _erect_ .

- Buildings are always determined by their _foundation_ .

- To _observe_ well is to _interpret_ well.

- We are always observing with a view to _interpreting_ and eventually _applying_ the _Scripture to observe_ .

- We can refer to the step of interpretation as the " _recreation_ " process. We are attempting to stand in the author's shoes and to recreate his experience.

- We are asking, "What did this mean _A then_ _____ ?" before we ever ask, "What does it mean to _us_ ?"

- It is impossible to apply the Word of God until you _understand_ it.

- Interpretation takes _time_, and it takes _skill_.

- Learning how to interpret the Bible does not mean we are going to _understand_ everything in it.

Five Principles of Interpretation

I. Principle #1: _Content_

- There is a cause/effect relationship between the _Content_ and its _meaning_.

- For the content, we employ the results of our _Observational_ studies. All of these provide us with the raw material with which we are going to _Provide Meaning / Interpret_ the Scriptures.

- The more time you spend in _observation_ the less time you will spend in _interpretation_.

II. Principle #2: _Context_

- _Context_ always refers to that which goes before and that which follows. Any time we break into the middle of a passage, we always need to look at its _Context_.

- Every major _Cult_ is built on a violation of this principle.

- Whenever you study a passage, you need to examine the _Verse before & after (Neighboring Verses_

[END OF SESSION FOUR]

Note: Principles of Interpretation #3, 4, and 5 will be covered in the next session.

WORKING IN THE BOOK

LEVEL ONE: Let's Get Started

1. Spend some time observing Mark 5:24-34, using the principles of observation that you learned in Sessions Two and Three. What is the immediate context of this passage?

2. What is the context of Mark 5:24-34 in terms of...

    • Christ's life and ministry?

    • the New Testament?

    • the entire Bible?

3. Briefly summarize what value you think each of these contexts might have in understanding Mark 5:24-34.

LEVEL TWO: For Those Who Want More

1. Turn to Hebrews 11 and select at least three different Old Testament characters mentioned there. Using a concordance, determine as much as you can about the historical context of their lives as the Bible reveals it. How does this information affect your understanding of Hebrews 11? How does it affect the statement that immediately follows Hebrews 11 in Hebrews 12:1-2?

2. Examine the context of Acts 1:1-8, placing it where it belongs in the chain of events from Jesus' crucifixion to His ascension into heaven. What impact does this context make on properly understanding this passage? What

major event follows the ascension that needs to be included in one's explanation of the historical context of Acts 1:1-8?

3. Based on the overall context of Acts 1:1-8, why do you think the disciples asked the Lord the question in verse 6? How does this context affect your understanding of verses 7-8?

LEVEL THREE: Building Beyond the Foundation

1. Read the Book of Jonah and see if you can discover the historical context of this book in relation to the nation of Israel? (Hint: see 2 Kings 14:25.)

2. Using whatever Bible study tools you have available (concordance, Bible handbook, atlas), what can you discover about the nation of Assyria during the time of Jonah? What were the Assyrians like politically, militarily, socially, and religiously? How does this expanded context help you better understand Jonah?

3. Can Jonah's reaction in chapter 4 be understood apart from the context of this episode? Why or why not?

4. Why is context important in relation to the following verses?

    • Romans 7:24

    • 1 Corinthians 6:9-10

    • James 2:24

SESSION FIVE
COMPARISON, CULTURE, & CONSULTATION

PREPARING FOR THE BOOK

STEP ONE: Open Mind

- "Private interpretation never meant that individuals have the right to distort the Scriptures. With the right of private interpretation comes the sober responsibility of accurate interpretation. Private interpretation gives us license to interpret, not to distort." —*R. C. Sproul*

- "The Bible is God's chart for you to steer by, to keep you from the bottom of the sea, and to show you where the harbor is, and how to reach it without running on rocks or bars."—*Henry Ward Beecher*

- "For everything that was written in the past was written to teach us, so that through endurance and the encouragement of the Scriptures we might have hope."—*Romans 15:4*

- "There's no better book with which to defend the Bible than the Bible itself." —*D. L. Moody*

- "What you bring away from the Bible depends to some extent on what you carry to it." —*Oliver Wendell Holmes*

STEP TWO: Open Heart

- "The study of God's Word brings peace to the heart. In it, we find a light for every darkness, life in death, the promise of our Lord's return, and the assurance of everlasting glory."—*D.L. Moody*

- "Deal with your servant according to your love and teach me your decrees." —*Psalm 119:124*

- "The Bible is like a telescope. If a man looks through his telescope, then he sees worlds beyond; but if he looks at his telescope, then he does not see anything but that. The Bible is a thing to be looked through, to see that which is beyond; but most people only look at it; and so they see only the dead letter." —*Phillips Brooks*

- "Sanctify them in the truth; Thy word is truth."—*John 17:17*

STEP THREE: Open Book

Now that you are well into the second step of Bible study, Interpretation, you may have noticed that in asking and answering questions to interpret the biblical text, you never have to move very far away from the text. In other words, just as you make observations by asking questions and letting the text answer them, so you engage in interpretation by asking questions and letting the text answer them, as well.

Over the years, believers have sometimes been very good at asking what the Scriptures mean. But far too often, they have settled on interpretations based on personal opinion, popular consensus, gut feelings, the persuasiveness of an argument, and even pooled ignorance. But as we'll see, the primary way to understand Scripture is by letting Scripture interpret Scripture.

How do we do that? By taking our questions to the text first and foremost, and by letting the Bible—in context—give us answers wherever possible. This is not simply a matter of finding "proof texts" to back up our preconceived notions. It means discovering the great unity and consistency of Scripture in regard to all that it addresses. That sometimes involves hard work, but it is work well invested.

In the last session, we looked at two important principles of interpretation—content and context. In this session, Dr. Hendricks will explain three more principles for determining the meaning of God's Word.

LOOKING TO THE BOOK

[BEGIN SESSION FIVE]

Introduction

- Interpretation asks and answers the question, "What does it _____?"

- Review:

- The first principle of interpretation is _____. That is, what do we discover in the process of _____ that will provide a basis for intelligent and accurate _____?

- The second principle of interpretation is _____ _____. That is, what goes _____and what_____?

Five Principles of Interpretation (cont.)

III. Principle #3: _____

- This means comparing _____ with _____. The great interpreter of Scripture is _____ itself.

> "You very rarely have to go outside of the Bible to explain anything in the Bible." —Donald Grey Barnhouse

- The _____ of the Bible take on meaning in light of the _____.

- Although the Bible was written by more than _____ different _____, the 66 books are ultimately the result of _____.

• The principle of comparison points up our need for a
_____. This provides a tool whereby
we can chase down _____.

    Example: "Believe"

1.

2.a.

  b.

  c.

IV. Principle #4: _____ **and**
_____**background**

• The key to studying the Bible is to set it against its
_____.

    Example: Ruth

• Our problem is that we tend to _____
that period of time our _____.

V. Principle #5: _____

• This refers to using _____
in our study of the Bible.

• As a carpenter-friend of mine said, "The more tools an
individual has, usually the better a _____
he is." This is also true in Bible study.

• The order is important: First _____;
then _____.

FIVE HELPFUL TOOLS

1._____

- A good study Bible has no _____. But it may have wide _____, and cross-_____ you can use in the process of comparison.

- Once you have a good study Bible, do not hesitate to _____ in it.

2._____

- You should keep an exhaustive concordance right on your_____ while you are studying. Two good concordances are _____'s and _____'s.

3._____

- In recent years, as a result of _____ discovery, more light has been shed on the Scriptures.

TOOLS OF THE TRADE

- A unique dictionary dealing with the language of the New Testament is *Vine's Expository Dictionary of New Testament Words.*

- Another good Bible dictionary is *The New Bible Dictionary*, edited by J.D. Douglas.

- A Bible dictionary is arranged _____ so it is easy to look up biblical terms.

4._____

- A handbook goes book-by-book through the entire Bible and provides all kinds of _____ material.

TOOLS OF THE TRADE

An excellent example of a Bible handbook is *Eerdman's Bible Handbook.*

- If you have _____, you should teach them to use these _____.

5. _____

- The Bible and its geography is a huge _____ spot in our culture.

TOOLS OF THE TRADE

A good example of a Bible atlas is the *Moody Atlas of Bible Lands.*

[END OF SESSION FIVE]

WORKING IN THE BOOK

LEVEL ONE: Let's Get Started

1. Explain in your own words why it is important to compare Scripture with Scripture.

2. How might your understanding of Revelation 2:7, 11, 17, and 29; and 3:5, 12, and 21 be helped by comparing those verses with 1 John 5:4-5?

3. Using a concordance, list other passages with which Hebrews 11:31-33 might be compared in order to gain a greater understanding of the kind of faith this chapter is discussing.

4. Name two portions of Scripture that you think you would better understand if you had a grasp of their cultural and historical backgrounds.

5. What situation described in John 4:27 can be explained by an understanding of ancient Near Eastern culture?

6. Visit a library or Christian bookstore and familiarize yourself with each of the following kinds of Bible study resources:

    • Study Bibles

    • An exhaustive concordance

    • Bible dictionaries

    • Bible handbooks

- Bible atlases

- Commentaries

How might each of these tools aid you in the step of Interpretation?

LEVEL TWO: For Those Who Want More

1. Compare the following pairs of verses and explain how they complement or explain each other:

   - Genesis 37:9-10 with Revelation 12:1

   - John 1:1-14 with 1 John 4:2-3

   - Genesis 3:15b with Matthew 27:33

   - Psalm 110:1 with Mark 16:19 and Hebrews 10:11-13.

2. In what ways would an understanding of cultural or historical background be helpful in understanding the following passages?

   - Ephesians 6:10-17

   - Song of Solomon 7:4-5

   - Mark 7:24-30

   - Romans 14:1-8

NOTES

3. Using each of the Bible study tools listed above (or as many as possible), see if you can find at least one informative insight per tool for each of the passages below:

   • Genesis 32:24-32

   • Ruth 3:1-18

   • 1 Samuel 15:1-29

   • Song of Solomon 7:4-5

   • 1 Corinthians 8:1-8

   • Revelation 1:9-11

LEVEL THREE: Building Beyond the Foundation

1. By comparing Scripture with Scripture, answer the following questions:

   • In light of Genesis 3:15, why was it important that Jesus be born of a virgin, as recorded in Matthew 1:23-25?

   • Read 2 Samuel 7:16 and explain the significance of the genealogies of Jesus found in Matthew 1:1-17 and Luke 3:23-38. How does this explain what many people called Him (as in Matthew 20:30-31)? Why do you think the two genealogies are slightly different?

2. By researching the cultural and historical background, answer the following questions:

   • Describe the scene in the city of Jerusalem on the day of Pentecost, when the events of Acts 2:1-13 took place. Why were so many people there? Why are so many countries mentioned in verses 9-11? (For a note of comparison, why is this event significant, in light of Genesis 9?)

   • In light of fishing practices on the Sea of Galilee, what was especially unusual about the events of John 21:36? Why?

   • What do you think was happening in Corinth, according to 1 Corinthians 1:11-13? Do you think this situation was unique to Paul's day? Why or why not?

3. Using each of the Bible study tools listed above (or as many as possible), see if you can find at least one informative insight per tool for each of the passages below:

   • 1 Samuel 4:1-11

   • Nehemiah 1

   • Luke 2:1-20

   • John 4:7-30

   • Acts 16:1-13

   • Revelation 2:12-17

NOTES

APPLICATION
How Does It Work?

SESSION SIX
THE WORKING WORD

PREPARING FOR THE BOOK

STEP ONE: Open Mind

- "Being confident of this, that he who began a good work in you will carry it on to completion until the day of Christ Jesus." —*Philippians 1:6*

- "Every revelation of God is a demand, and the way to knowledge of God is by obedience."—*William Temple*

- "'For my thoughts are not your thoughts, neither are your ways my ways,' declares the Lord." —*Isaiah 55:8*

- "We must observe that the knowledge of God which we are invited to cultivate is not that which, resting satisfied with empty speculation, only flutters in the brain; but a knowledge which will prove substantial and fruitful whenever it is duly perceived and rooted in the heart." —*John Calvin*

- "But prove yourselves doers of the word, and not merely hearers who delude themselves." —*James 1:22*

STEP TWO: Open Heart

- "A man's heart is right when he wills what God wills." —*Thomas Aquinas*

- "Does the Lord delight in burnt offerings and sacrifices as much as in obeying the voice of the Lord? To obey is better than sacrifice, and to heed is better than the fat of rams." —*1 Samuel 15:22*

- "No book will make you grow like the Bible." —*George Sweeting*

- Sow a thought, and you reap an act;
  Sow an act, and you reap a habit;
  Sow a habit, and you reap a character;
  Sow a character, and you reap a destiny. —*Anonymous*

- "The man who is too old to learn was probably always too old to learn." —*Henry Haskins*

- "Teach me to do your will, for you are my God; may your good Spirit lead me on level ground." —*Psalm 143:10*

STEP THREE: Open Book

As Dr. Hendricks has pointed out, it is impossible to come to the Scriptures diligently and intelligently without running head-on into the need for application. Hebrews 4:12 puts it this way: "The word of God is living and active. Sharper than any double-edged sword, it penetrates even to dividing soul and spirit, joints and marrow; it judges the thoughts and attitudes of the heart."

So before moving into the crucial step of Application, why not pause for a time of review and reflection? Are you ready for God's Word to cut deeply into your own life, to lay bare the hidden places of your heart, and to do its work of convicting, convincing, and converting your mind in any and every area? The spirit of Bible study is a willing heart—and the fruit of Bible study is a changed life.

One more suggestion to consider: If you have not yet begun to keep a personal journal or notebook of your Bible study process, now would be a good time to start. Nothing fancy, mind you—just a way of keeping track of the passages of Scripture you study and how God touches your life through them. Logging your spiritual progress day-by-day will not only reinforce what God is teaching you at the time, it will give you a valuable resource to go back to in the future.

Now—on to Application!

NOTES

LOOKING TO THE BOOK

[BEGIN SESSION SIX]

Introduction

- Application asks and answers the question, "How does it _Does Work_?"

- The Bible was not written to satisfy our curiosity; it was written to _transform your life_

- The ultimate goal of Bible study is not to do something to _for the Bible_, but to allow _Bible_ to do something to _for you_.

> "Too often we come to God's Word to study it, to teach it,
> to preach it, to outline it—to do everything in the world
> with it except be changed by it."

- Our task as Christians is first to get into the _Word of God_; then, second, to allow the _the word of God_ to get into _us_.

- Spiritual growth is a _process_ of change.

A Four-Step Process of Spiritual Change

1. _Know_
2. _Relate (the truth of God to our lives)_
3. _Meditate (lost art)_
4. _Practice_

Insight (handwritten)

I. Step #1: _____

A. You have to know the _*interpretation*_ .

- The _*interp applied*_ is always based on the _*application*_ .

  If the _*interpretation*_ is erroneous, the _____ will be erroneous.

  If the _____ is correct, you have a possibility that the _____ will be correct.

- Key idea:

  Interpretation is _____ ;
  Application is _____ .

B. You have to know the _*interpretation*_ .

> "Take *heed to yourself* and to your teaching."
> —1 Timothy 4:1

- Knowing yourself involves...

  - knowing your _*assets*_ , and...

  - knowing your _*liabilities*_ .

  - If you know your _*assets*_ , it will develop your _*liabilities*_ .

  If you know your _*liability*_ , they will develop your _*faith*_ .

> "For by the grace given me I say to every one of you: Do not think of yourself more highly than you ought, but rather think of yourself with sober judgment. . . ." —Romans 12:3

NOTES

Christian Growth is a Process

Christ
home
sex life
Social
Business (Profession life)
Community

II. Step #2: Relate

- We need to relate the Word of God to our experience.
- Christianity is best understood as a series of new new relationships

> *"Therefore, if any man be in Christ, he is a new creation; the old has gone, the new has come!" —2 Corinthians 5:17*

- Christian growth is a process; but it is a dynamic process.

THE WORKING WORD

- A new relationship to God (my father).
- A new relationship to Self (new self image)
- A new relationship to other people.
- A new relationship to enemy (satan).

HOW THE WORD OF GOD AFFECTS OUR RELATIONSHIPS:

- We find passages that expose my sin.
- We find passages that God will give promise.
- We find passages that commands.
- We find passages that examples.
- The Christian life is not impossible, it's super natural! It's a ________ life.

> *"Ask yourself this simple question: What is there in your life that you cannot explain on any other basis other than the supernatural?"*

[END OF SESSION SIX]

Note: Steps #3 and 4 will be covered in the next session.

NOTES

[handwritten margin notes:]
- Change regime
- humility
- this climate people must adopt change
- challenge how do you stay the course and accomplish the goal

Whatever you

2. we all have a mission - to serve God

Acts 17

Ways we progress in our faith
Kidner
Joy
fruit
submitting to christ
trusting him more

Gal. 5
Fruits of the Spirit - know
goal

WORKING IN THE BOOK

LEVEL ONE: Let's Get Started

1. In your opinion, why do believers resist change in their lives? How does this hinder the application of Scripture?
Everyone resists changes in how they accomplish a task. Minds are not always accepting of doing things differently

2. What is the goal of God's work in our lives, according to Romans 8:29? What do you think this will involve?
Goal to be come like him. Knowing what Gods in guiding us to do & doing it correctly

3. Describe the relationship between accurate interpretation and correct application. How would you sum this up in one sentence? *Know what to do and do it correctly*
James 4:17

4. What is Paul's point in 1 Timothy 4:16? What does this require of us in our study of Scripture? *Know what to do set ex ample for others*

5. Based on 2 Corinthians 5:17, list several areas of your life in which you have seen changes since trusting Christ as your Savior. Privately, list others in which you still need to see change. *Accepted Christ as a child have always tried to live by Christ's rules.*

LEVEL TWO: For Those Who Want More

What areas of life and relationships are addressed in the following verses? What attitudes or actions are commanded (be as specific as possible)?

- Ephesians 4:31-32
  Get rid of all action that are counter to Gods guidance bitterness, rage, brawling, slander, Be Kind to one another

- Proverbs 15:16
  Better to live a simple God led life than to have plenty of everything & live in turmoil

- Titus 2:3-5

  Women are to teach young women; love their husband & children, self controlled, busy at home

- Ephesians 5:5

  Be moral, pure, generous --- Not be in God's Kingdom

- James 3:2-12

  Don't use our tongue for immoral words. Instead use it to build up + bless others

LEVEL THREE: Building Beyond the Foundation

Carefully study each of the verses below, using the principles of Observation and Interpretation. Then list at least three points of personal application based on your study.

- Romans 8:28-32

  God works that those who love him will be blessed. He called us --- he will never leave us to fend for ourself.

- James 3:13-18

  Do good, Humility. Be humble. Do not be selfish

- Psalm 1:1-3

  God will provide our needs; We will lack for nothing. Trust in God for everything

- Genesis 22:1-12

- Proverbs 19:1-2

  accept blame for mistakes

SESSION SEVEN
THE WORD THAT WORKS

PREPARING FOR THE BOOK

STEP ONE: Open Mind

- "The Bible, God's inerrant Word, is forever true whether or not anyone reads or believes it; but it becomes of value to you when you get ahold of it for yourself. Never leave a passage of Scripture until it has said something to you." —*Robert A. Cook*

- "Many are the plans in a man's heart, but it is the Lord's purpose that prevails." —*Proverbs 19:21*

- "If a man's Bible is coming apart, it is an indication that he himself is fairly well put together." —*Anonymous*

STEP TWO: Open Heart

- "If Jesus Christ be God and died for me, then no sacrifice can be too great for me to make for Him." —*C.T. Studd*

- "And. . .they began dragging Jason and some brethren before the city authorities, shouting, 'These men who have upset the world have come here also. . .!'" —*Acts 17:6*

STEP THREE: Open Book

In the last session, Dr. Hendricks suggested that the Christian life is best understood as a series of new relationships. Here's a suggestion for helping you apply the Word of God to the various relationships in your life.

In your journal or notebook, make a list of four categories of people: (1) your family and relatives; (2) Christian friends and associates with whom you are close (for example, people in your local church); (3) Christians with whom you are familiar but do not have a close, ongoing relationship (for example, missionaries that you support, teachers or authors whom you admire, or leaders of Christian churches and ministries); and (4) non-Christians, especially those with whom you have a relationship.

You can use those lists to do two things. First, you can make it a basis for prayer, mentioning specific people by name. As you do, ask God not only to work in the person's life, but also to give you insight and awareness as to how Christ wants to affect your relationship with that person.

A second way to use the list is to review it in connection with your application of Scripture. When you come to a command, a promise, a condition, a pattern—ask yourself: "Is there someone in my life who would be affected if I practiced this spiritual truth in my life?"

Now let's turn to Dr. Hendricks' final session on the application of biblical truth.

NOTES

Behind in your Church tavie

Prov 23:7

what you think you are.

Meditation — feling Mend w/ what God want us to do

Psalm 19

Phil 2:14

LOOKING TO THE BOOK

[BEGIN SESSION SEVEN]

A FOUR-STEP PROCESS OF SPIRITUAL CHANGE *(cont.)*

- Review:

  - Application involves. . .

    Step #1: *Know*

    Step #2: *Relate to god, yourself & other*

III. Step #3: *meditate — essential to application*

- Joshua 1:8

  Notice the relationship between *Meditation* and *Successful / Prosperity* *action*

- Proverbs 23:7

  The basic principle here is that you *~~reap~~* *are* what you *think* ~~sow~~.

- Psalm 1:1-2

  One of the fastest ways to *Mediter Spiritual stability* your life is through *meditation*.

- Psalm 119:97

  This shows us that *meditation* involves using our *time w/ God wisely . memory highest wisdom memory* is always linked with *brain*, *that* provides the mind with *fuel* needed to make *meditation* profitable.

TOOLS OF THE TRADE

- *The Topical Memory System,* by The Navigators

IV. Step #4: _practice_

- This is the ultimate goal of _application_.

- The task of Bible study is not to _fatten_ _geese_, but to train _athletes_ and equip _soldiers for the_ _realities of life_.

- Anytime you study the Scriptures, ask, "Lord, how can this truth _transform_ my life in specific areas?"

- Our _hunger_ for the Word of God will be in direct proportion to our _obedience_ to the Word of God.

NINE QUESTIONS FOR APPLICATION

1. Is there a _is there any example_ to _for me to follow_?

2. Is there a _any sin that God wants me_ to _avoid_?

3. Is there a _any promise_ to _claim_?

4. Is there a _any prayer for me_ to _repeat_?

5. Is there a _any command_ to _to obey_?

6. Is there a _condition_ to _to meet_?

---

7. Is there a *Any Verse*

 to *Memorize* ?

8. Is there a *Error*

 to *Mark* ?

9. Is there a *Challenge*

 to *face* ?

- Before the Word of God can bring change to my world, it must first bring change to my *life* .

- The Bible is not God's Word because it *works* ; it *works* because it's God's Word!

[END OF SESSION SEVEN]

WORKING IN THE BOOK

LEVEL ONE: Let's Get Started

1. Contrast the Bible's concept of meditation with the world's concept. What is the main difference?

2. What would be Joshua's key to success, according to Joshua 1:8? What response did this process require of Joshua? What does this reveal about the process of meditating on Scripture? *Think on it ~~not~~ dwell on it (mentally).*

3. Describe the relationship between meditation and godliness in light of Psalm 1:1-2. What attitude toward God's Word does this passage describe? How do you think the psalmist arrived at this attitude? *By wrapping our minds and hearts around Gods word. by doing so we have peace + joy.*

4. In regard to spending time meditating in the Scriptures, what obstacles do you personally face? What solutions can you find to these obstacles?

5. Pick three verses of Scripture and memorize them this week.

6. Review the nine questions of application in regard to some of the biblical texts you have been studying as a part of this course. In what areas and by what means do you need to start practicing biblical truth?

NOTES

meditation you
Ps 119:15 Precepts
78 Precepts
97

LEVEL TWO: For Those Who Want More

1. Use a concordance to trace the words *meditate* and *meditation* through the Bible. What insights does this study yield?

2. Study Psalm 119 and list as many benefits of meditation as you can find.

3. Pick a psalm and memorize it this week.

4. Find at least five passages that emphasize the need to practice the truth of Scripture.

5. Spend some time meditating on Ephesians 5:15-16, then list no fewer than six ways in which you can practice this advice in your own life. *Be careful how you live Be wise but unwise, make the most of every opportunity*

LEVEL THREE: Building Beyond the Foundation

Study Philippians 2:1-18 using the principles of Observation and Interpretation. Then do the following:

1. List as many direct commands from this passage as you can find. Summarize each in a one- to three-word statement. *be united w/Christ*

2. For each command, briefly summarize the rationale, the reason, or the resource for carrying it out (according to the context in Philippians 2).

3. For each command, summarize what you think would be the most common objection made by someone who needs to practice its application in his or her life.

4. Going back to question #2, answer the objections for each point of application.

5. For each command, give at least two examples of practical ways in which it could be applied in your own life.

LIVING BY THE BOOK
LEADER'S GUIDE

INTRODUCTION

For more than fifty years, Dr. Howard G. Hendricks has been teaching Bible study methods to budding pastors, missionaries, and other Christian leaders at Dallas Theological Seminary. The principles taught by Dr. Hendricks have become legendary. So it only made sense to ask Dr. Hendricks if he would mind videotaping the core of his material for the benefit of those who may never attend seminary, but who want to know how to get into Scripture for themselves.

Dr. Hendricks was overjoyed by that prospect. He saw it as an opportunity to fulfill his long-standing desire to see God's people gain a firsthand acquaintance with the revealed Word of God. As he puts it, "The great tragedy in Evangelicalism today is that many Christians are under the Word of God, but they are not *in* it for themselves."

However, in producing this video series, Dr. Hendricks was keenly aware that he would only be getting the ball rolling. What was needed, he felt, were leaders who would be committed to helping viewers actually get started in the process of personal Bible study.

That's where you come into play. Dr. Hendricks, as well as the rest of us at Living By The Book, see you as an indispensable partner in making this series effective. Your role is to "shepherd" participants along—encouraging, explaining, motivating, sometimes even nudging—whatever it takes to help people discover the joy of delving into the Word for themselves.

You have a unique opportunity. This Leader's Guide is designed to help you in your task.

GETTING STARTED

Once your church or group has made the decision to use the "Living By The Book" series, you need to establish a schedule or format. The series was designed for use in a variety of settings, from Sunday school classes to small group Bible studies to discipleship groups. Each session has been edited to 25 minutes or less in order to leave time for group discussion and interaction. The seven sessions are divided as follows:

OBSERVATION

Session One: An Overview of the Process

Session Two: Learning to Look, Learning to Read

Session Three: Learning What to Look For

INTERPRETATION

Session Four: Content & Context

Session Five: Comparison, Culture, & Consultation

APPLICATION

Session Six: The Working Word

Session Seven: The Word That Works

The three major sections—Observation, Interpretation, and Application—can be treated as separate modules. However, we strongly recommend that you take these modules in the order given, as Dr. Hendricks' method proceeds from Observation to Interpretation to Application.

These sessions can be adapted to meet many different schedules. But perhaps the most effective approach is to present the sessions over seven successive weeks. That way, participants can plan on a seven-week course, with perhaps an eighth week added for review.

No matter how you adapt the series to meet your needs and time requirements, remember that the key to effectiveness is planning and preparation, coupled with an exciting and stimulating presentation that draws participants into each session.

SETTING THE STAGE

After you have determined a schedule, your real work begins. Start by informing the leadership of your church or group and enlist their support. This is crucial if your efforts are to be successful.

The next thing to do is to publicize the program in as many ways and places as possible. Consider showing prospective participants the first few minutes of Session One, which establishes the need for Bible study. Sunday school classes or a Sunday night service are ideal forums in which to build momentum for the series.

If possible, determine ahead of time the actual number of people who are planning to participate in the program. That way, you can order enough workbooks so that each participant will have one. The workbook promotes learning and increases the probability that people will actually start studying the Bible. Be sure to give yourself enough time for the workbooks to arrive before the first session begins.

CONDUCTING THE SESSIONS

1. Before each session, prepare yourself by praying for yourself and for those who will participate in the "Living By The Book" program. Then preview the recorded session and the material in the workbook. Remember, the workbook has been designed for people with different levels of experience in Bible study, so adjust your use of this tool to challenge each of your participants at the appropriate level.

2. Prepare the room where the session will be held. Make sure you have enough seats, and consider using tables so that participants have a hard surface to write on. Make sure you have the proper equipment to screen the session, and check ahead of time to make sure that equipment

is in good working order. If you are expecting a large crowd (more than 30 people), consider using more than one monitor, so that everyone can view the session comfortably. You want to make it easy for participants to see and hear what Dr. Hendricks has to say, in order to encourage their participation.

3. Use the session plans in this Leader's Guide merely as a guide. Don't be so rigid that you discourage participation. On the other hand, don't be so loose and flexible that you waste people's time. Get to know your people so that you can guide the discussion to profitable ends.

4. Encourage participants to complete at least one of the three levels indicated in the "Working in the Book" section of their workbooks. Suggest that they work together in small groups, or in pairs outside of class. Follow up to see who is completing the exercises, and whether anyone has questions or needs help.

5. Always begin and end the session promptly on time. Set expectations ahead of time for when the session will begin and end, and then live up to those expectations.

If you are prepared and enthusiastic, your attitude will infect the group and greatly increase the probability of life-changing results.

NOTES

SESSION PLAN OVERVIEW

In general, we suggest the following timetable for a one-hour session built around one of the video sessions in "Living By The Book."

INTRODUCTION (5-10 MINUTES)

Use this time to set a positive and encouraging atmosphere for the class. Handle any administrative details, such as filling out nametags, passing out workbooks, introducing visitors, and so forth. Begin with prayer, asking for God's wisdom and blessing as you learn to study His Word.

REVIEW AND PREPARATION (5-10 MINUTES)

Briefly summarize key points from any previous sessions, and ask for comments about the exercises completed. Answer questions as time permits. (Remember to be flexible in allowing time for real problems to be cleared up, but don't be distracted by side issues. Lengthy questions may need to be handled outside of class or in a special session.)

Challenge the class by reading from the "Preparing for the Book" portion of the workbook. Encourage each person to read that section before class every week.

RECORDED PRESENTATION (25 MINUTES)

Introduce the session for the week and start the recorded session. Encourage everyone to follow along in their workbooks, filling in the blanks and taking notes as they listen to Dr. Hendricks.

DISCUSSION (10-15 MINUTES)

Ask participants to review their notes, fill in any lingering blanks, and think about any particular insight or point that stood out to them. Use this time to emphasize key points that Dr. Hendricks has made in his presentation.

ASSIGNMENTS (5 MINUTES)

Encourage participants to determine which level of study is applicable to them, and tell them to complete the exercises in their workbooks during the coming week. Suggest that they study with a spouse or friend, or in a small group.

OBSERVATION

SESSION ONE: AN OVERVIEW OF THE PROCESS

As this is the first session, you should briefly explain to participants that "Living By The Book" is a course on Bible study methods. Dr. Hendricks points out that there are three steps to the process: Observation, Interpretation, and Application. Observation asks and answers the question, "What do I see?" Interpretation asks and answers the question, "What does it mean?" Application asks and answers the question, "How does it work?"

Session One looks at several reasons why people don't study the Bible, and then at three reasons why we must study the Bible. It also gives an overview of the Bible study process, and highlights four elements of what to look for in Observation.

You should walk participants through the course workbook, explaining each section and its purpose. Encourage them to choose the level of exercises that would be most appropriate for them. Where necessary, suggest the appropriate level.

SESSION TWO: LEARNING TO LOOK, LEARNING TO READ

Begin by briefly summarizing the key points from Session One, and ask for any comments or questions about the exercises.

In this session, Dr. Hendricks explains that learning to study the Bible begins with learning to read. He then gives three basic rules for reading.

NOTES

Before sending participants on their way, be sure to remind them to complete the exercises in their workbooks.

SESSION THREE: LEARNING WHAT TO LOOK FOR

Before starting the video, review the principal points covered so far. Make sure that participants understand the importance of the step of Observation. Remind them that the central question here is, "What does the biblical text say?"

In Session Three, Dr. Hendricks names six things to look for in the step of Observation. He uses the hand as a simple means of remembering these six. After the recorded session is finished, review this object lesson with participants, to help them lock the six points in their memory.

INTERPRETATION

SESSION FOUR: CONTENT & CONTEXT

This session takes participants into the second step of Bible study method, Interpretation. Before starting the recorded session, poll your group to see how they are coming along with their exercises. You might even have one or two group members say a few words about the impact of this material on their lives.

In Session Four, Dr. Hendricks focuses on two important aspects of Interpretation: content and context of a passage.

After the presentation, make sure that participants understand what is meant by Interpretation. Remind them that the central question for this step is, "What does the biblical text mean?"

SESSION FIVE: COMPARISON, CULTURE, & CONSULTATION

Start by reviewing what has been covered so far, particularly the two areas covered during the previous session, content and context. Ask participants for feedback as to how their exercises are coming along.

80

In Session Five, Dr. Hendricks covers three more aspects of Interpretation: comparison of Scripture with Scripture; the cultural and historical background; and consultation, the use of secondary sources. Concerning this last step, Dr. Hendricks highlights a number of Bible study tools during his presentation. Consider displaying some of those resources on a table, so that participants can peruse them afterward.

APPLICATION

SESSION SIX: THE WORKING WORD

This session is the first of two that deal with the final step of Bible study method, Application. Before starting the recorded session, review with participants the first two steps in the process—Observation and Interpretation. Remind them that in Application, the central question is, "How does this work?"

In Session Six, Dr. Hendricks introduces the crucial step of Application, and then gives an overview of a four-step process of applying God's Word. He then covers the first two steps in the process: knowing and relating.

After the recorded session is finished, have your group discuss the nature of Application, and why it so often fails to happen. Remind them of Dr. Hendricks' point that the question of Application is not "Does it work?" but, "How does it work?"

SESSION SEVEN: THE WORD THAT WORKS

Before starting the recorded session, review the step of Application with participants. See how they are doing in completing their exercises.

In Session Seven, Dr. Hendricks concludes the video series by looking at the last two steps in the four-step process of applying God's Word: meditation and practice.

After the recorded session has ended, discuss with participants the key points covered by Dr. Hendricks. If this is the last time that your group will be together for "Living

NOTES

By The Book," devote some time for group members to share what they have learned during the series, and how they intend to use what they have learned in the future. Allow time for prayer, asking God to help each participant become a faithful and effective student of the Word.

(If you wish, you can hold an eighth session to review the course material and clear up any lingering questions or problems that participants have.)

CPSIA information can be obtained at www.ICGtesting.com
Printed in the USA
LVOW09s0218160115

423070LV00009B/327/P

9 780982 575635